# The FOSS WALK
## by
## Mark W. Jones

Printed and published
by
Maxiprint, Kettlestring Lane, Clifton Moor,
York YO3 8XF. Telephone (0904) 692000

© Mark Jones 1994

# INTRODUCTION

The Foss is a modest little river. Probably half the population of York has no idea where it comes from, before it joins the Ouse in the city. Yet it's of great historic importance. The Romans, finding that it combined with the Ouse to provide a natural defence, decided to build here their fortress of Eboracum, and York took root. Recent excavations have proved that the Foss was later used in turn by the Anglo-Saxons and the Vikings for commerce.

In the 14th Century, the Merchant Adventurers built their Hall upon its banks; and around 1800 it was made navigable for some 12 miles, with the construction of the Pond Head reservoir near its source, to maintain water-levels. More recently it was used for many years for the transport of cocoa beans and other ingredients up to Rowntree's warehouse in Leetham's Mill. Historically, therefore, the Foss has every right to be proud of itself.

Our Foss Walk starts from its confluence with the Ouse. Thanks to the Rowntree Foundation's new walkway, we keep near our river through the city. Remarkably quickly, we reach a tree-lined riverside pathway that takes us out into the quiet countryside of the Vale of York; until, beyond Strensall, we find ourselves in a world of wide-skied remoteness. Then come the hills — gentle at first, but getting steeper and more wooded, until we reach at last the delectable lake at Pond Head, within a stone's throw of the source of the Foss. From there, it's all downhill (nearly) to the nearest, and attractive, market-town of Easingwold. For those with energy to spare, however, we've suggested an enjoyable digression to take in Coxwold.

This brief Guide is simply to help you along the way, whether on foot or in the mind's eye. It can't pretend to cover the wealth of history and natural history to be found (see "Some other publications"), though some of the visual attractions of the Walk have invaded the pages from time to time.
The Walk lends itself well to leisurely progress from place to place, by the supplementary use of local buses to get you back to wherever you started from. It's not intended as a challenge to the do-it-in-a-day slogger, and you can stay overnight en route, if you feel like it. And don't be put off by my recurrent references to mud. Few winters can be as soggy as the one in which this booklet has been written, tried and tested!

So may your weather match the pleasures of the Foss Walk itself.

Mark Jones
January 1988

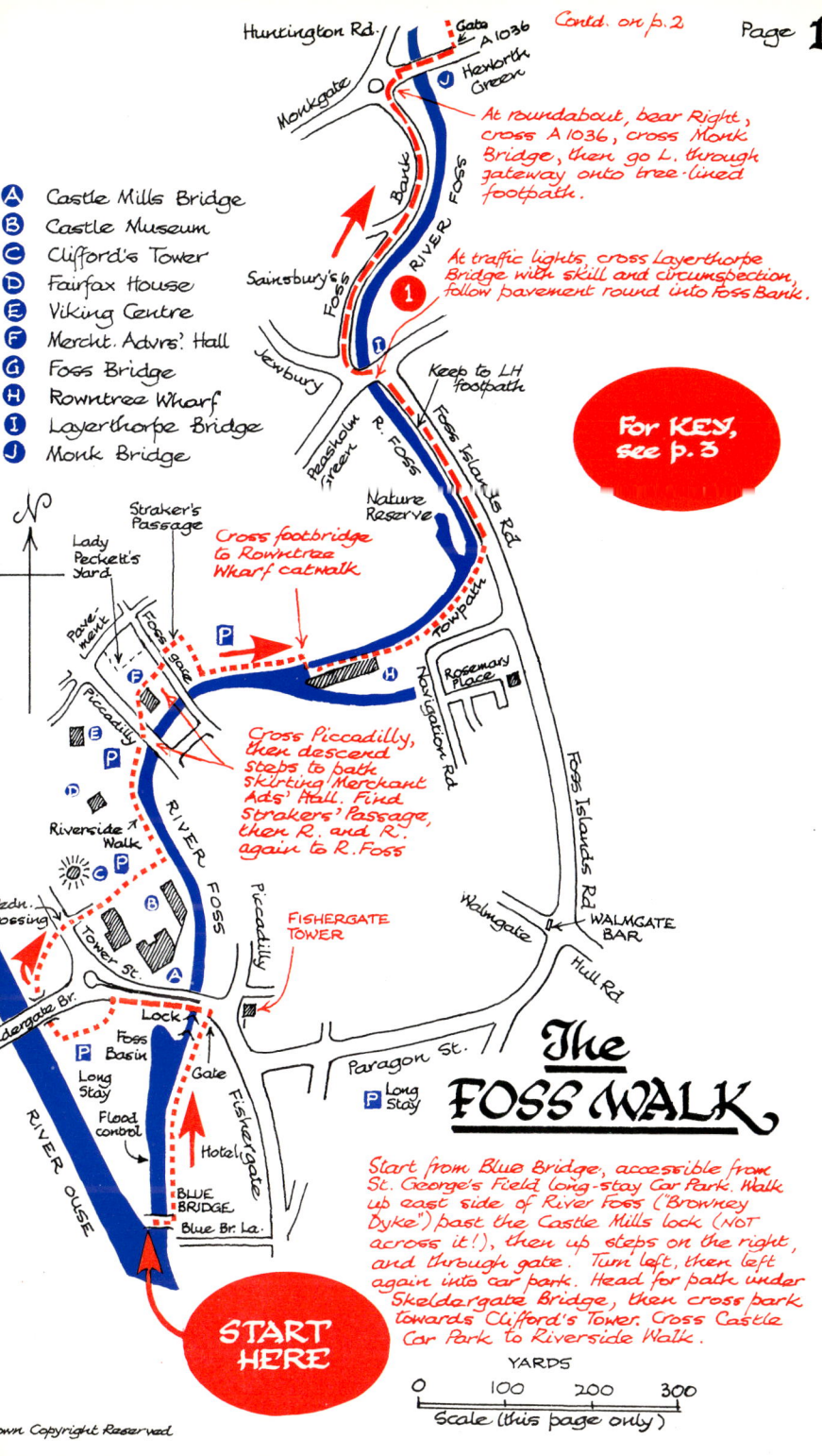

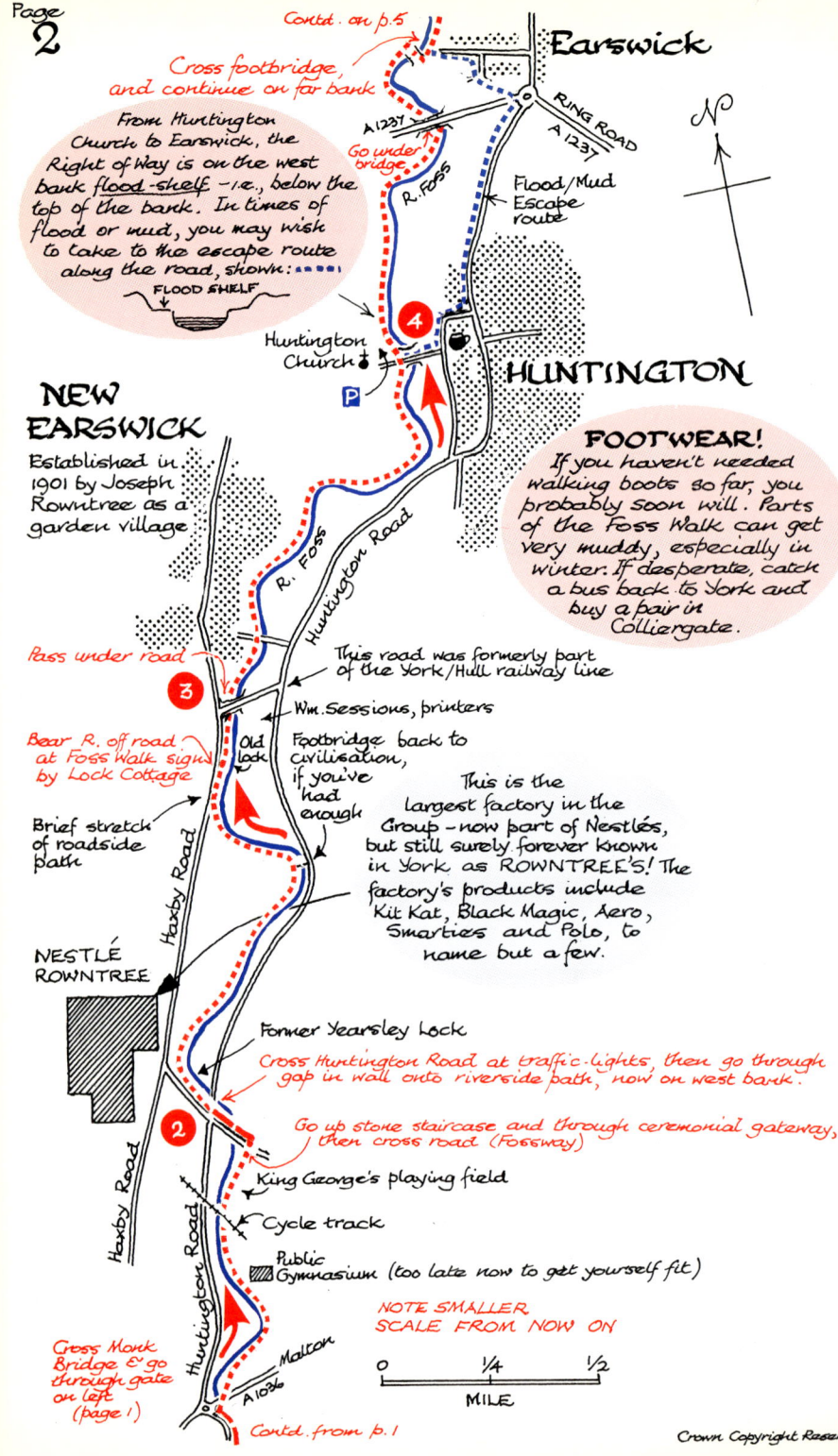

# Page 3

## KEY to your route

- ▪▪▪▪▪▪▪ Along footpath or bridleway
- ▬ ▬ ▬ Along or beside surfaced road
- ▪▪▪▪▪▪▪ Optional variations
- ═══════ Public roads
- ═══════ Farm roads
- ← Direction of Walk as described
- (15) Approx. miles from Blue Bridge

- 🍺 Favoured Pub
- ⛪ Church with tower/spire
- 🌲 Woodland
- ∿ Rivers
- ⬬ Lakes and ponds

*Instructions are in red italics\**
← Arrow relating to instruction\*
← " " " anything else

**\* but blue during digressions**

The Foss and Huntington Church (p.2)  MWJ

Farlington (p.7)  MWJ

Page 4

A FEW FOSS WALK RESIDENTS*

Hawker Dragonfly

Kingfisher

Himalayan Balsam

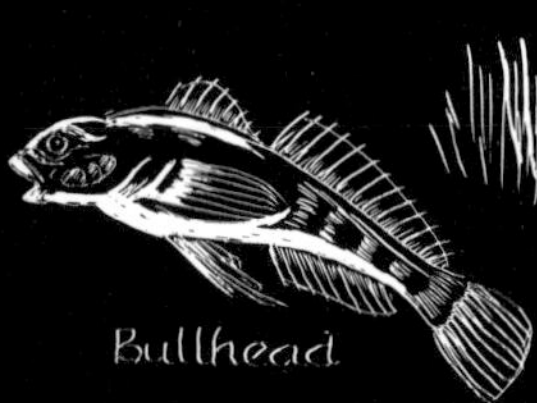

Bullhead

Heron

Nine-spined Stickleback

*See also pages 7, 9, 10 and back cover

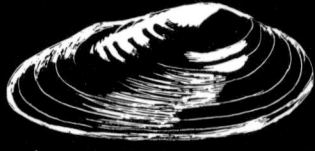

Fresh-water Mussel

MWJ

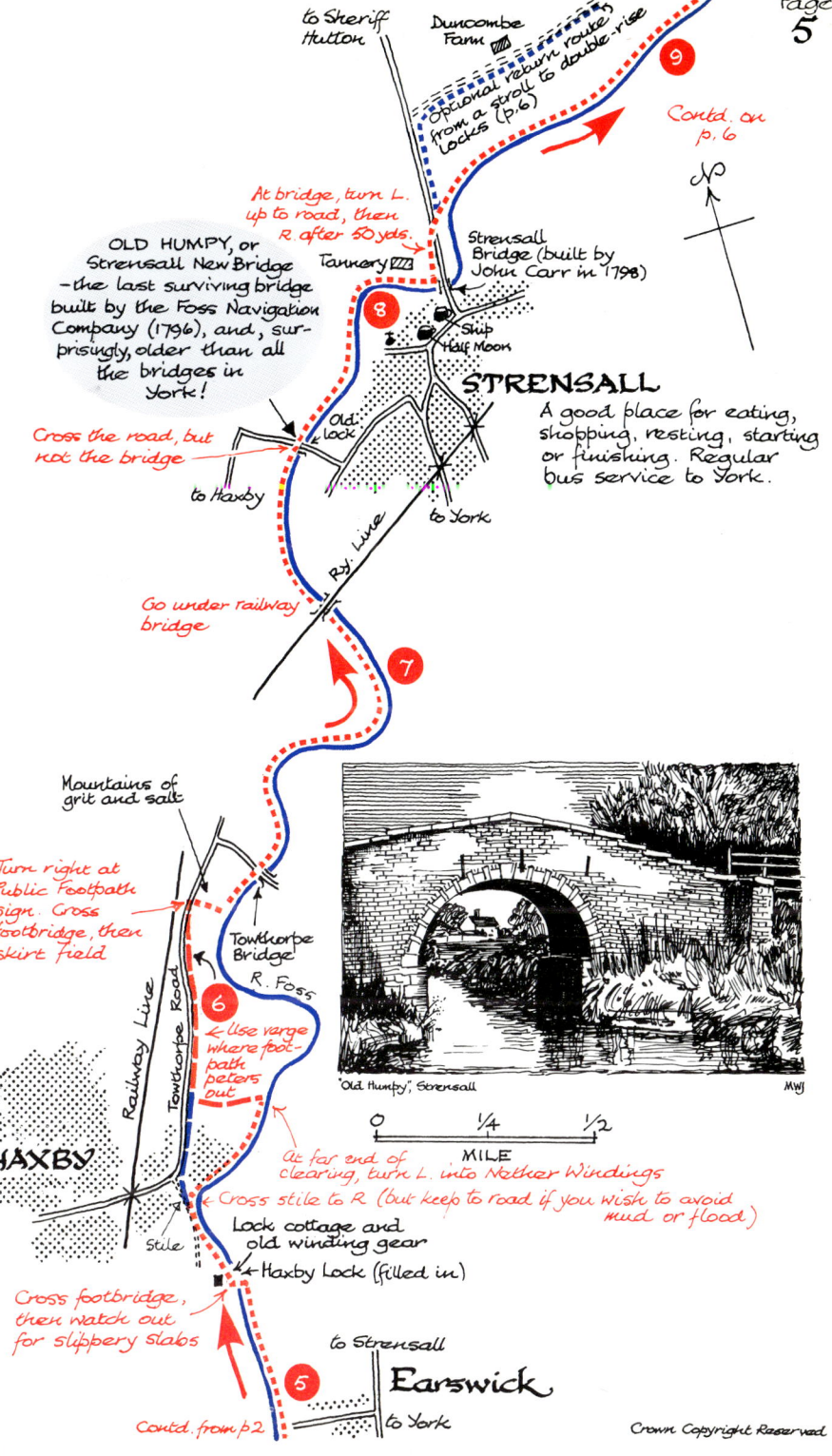

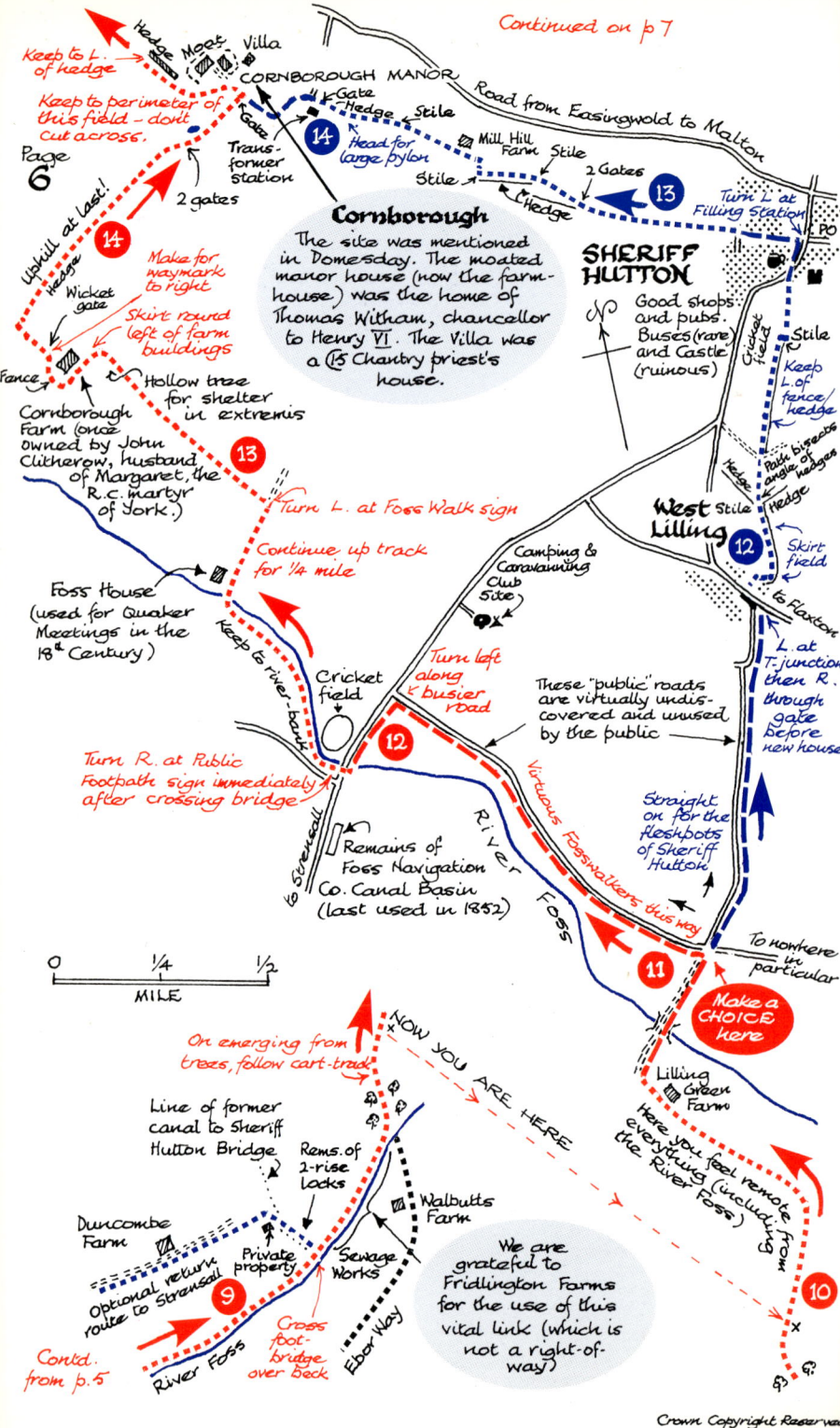

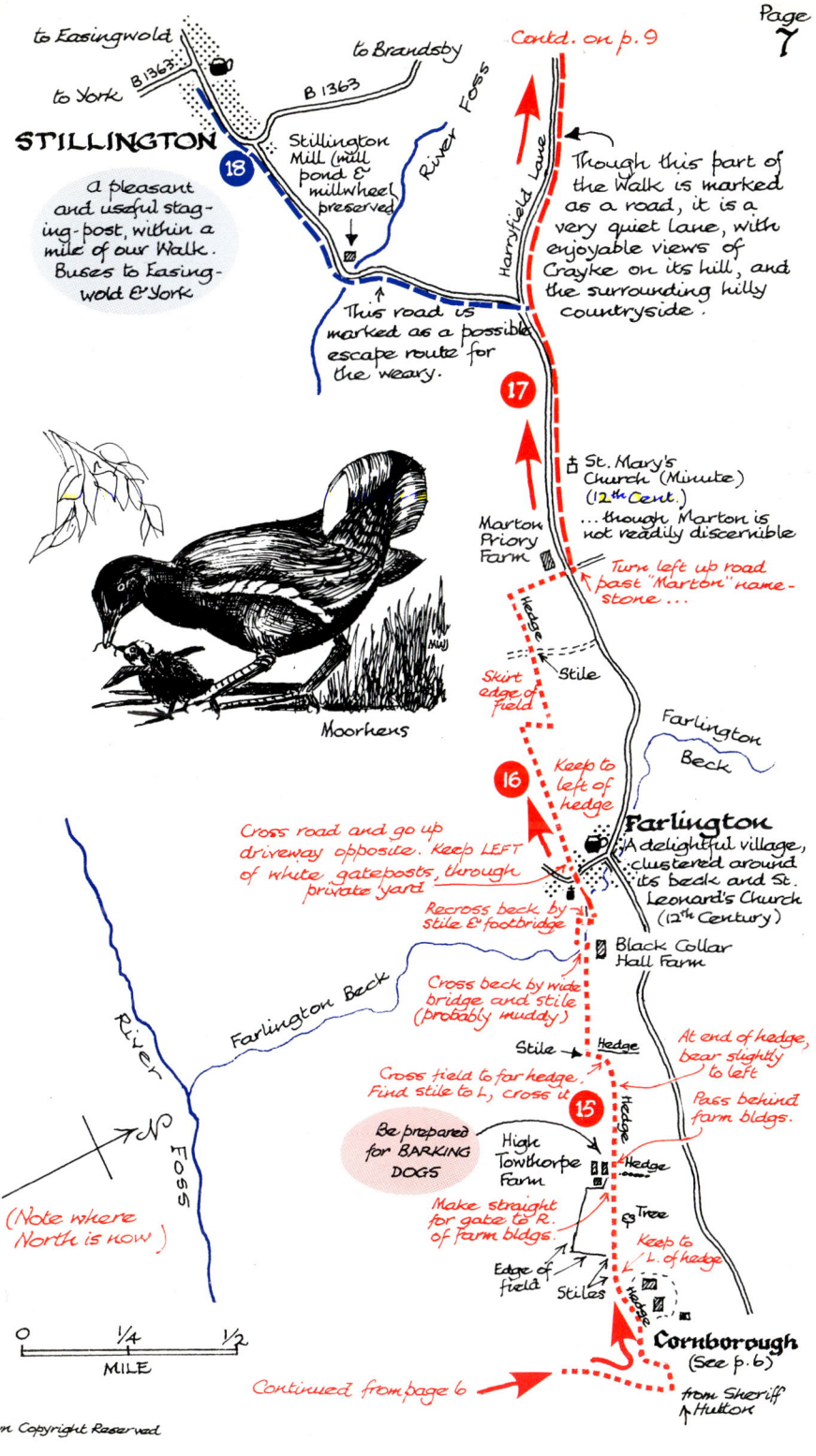

Page 8

Crayke (p.9)　　　MWJ

Coxwold (p.10)　　　MWJ

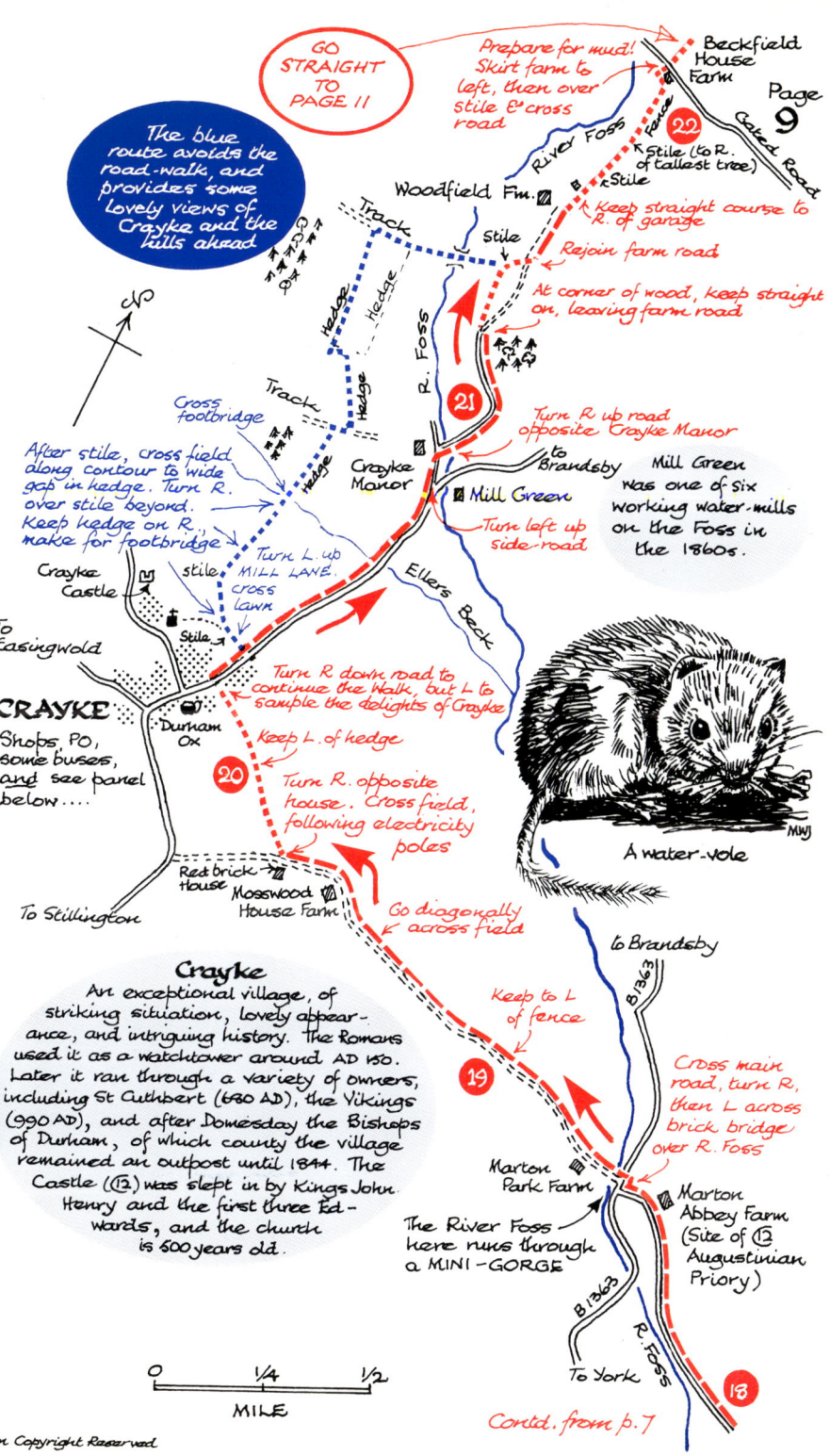

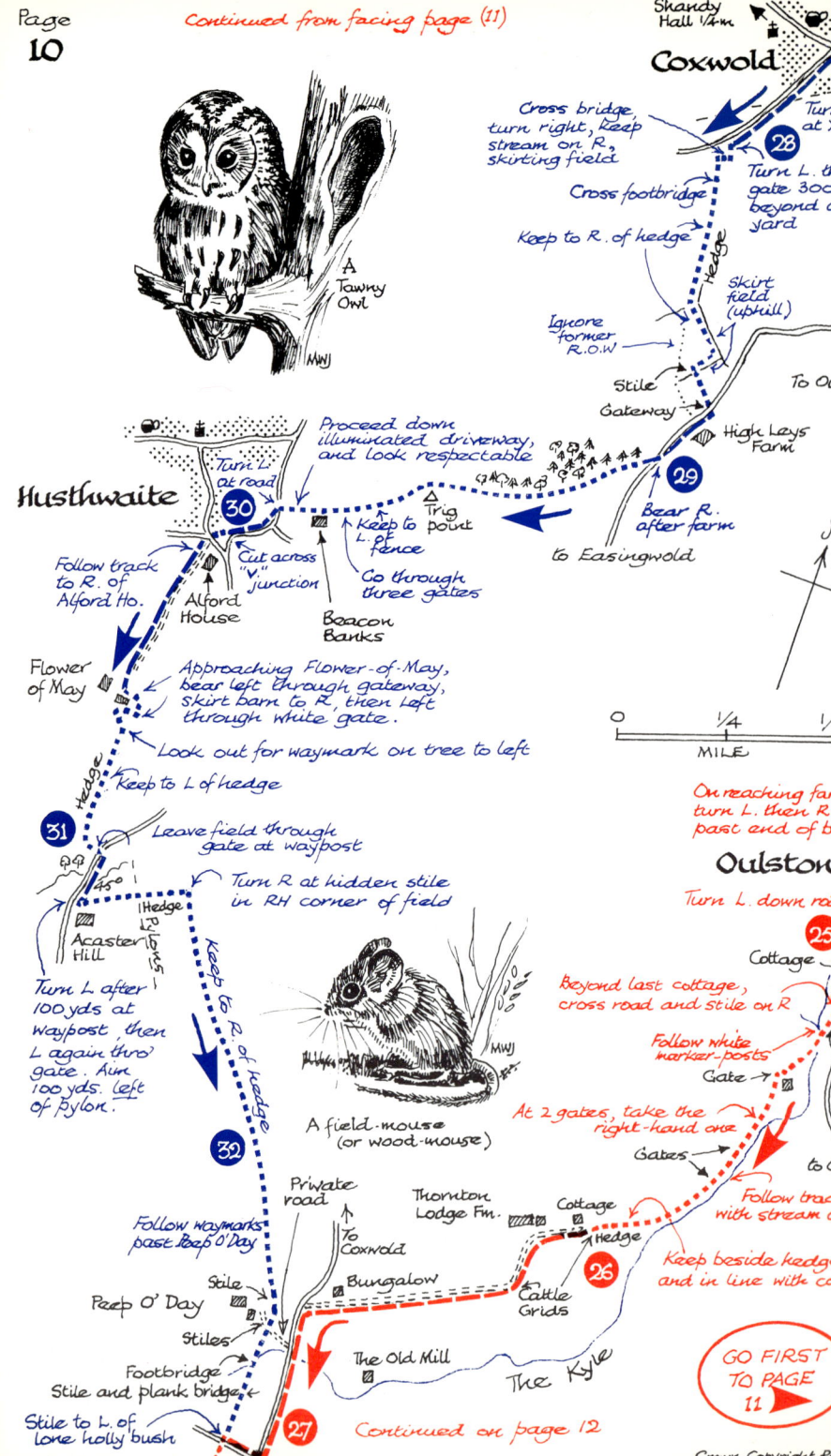

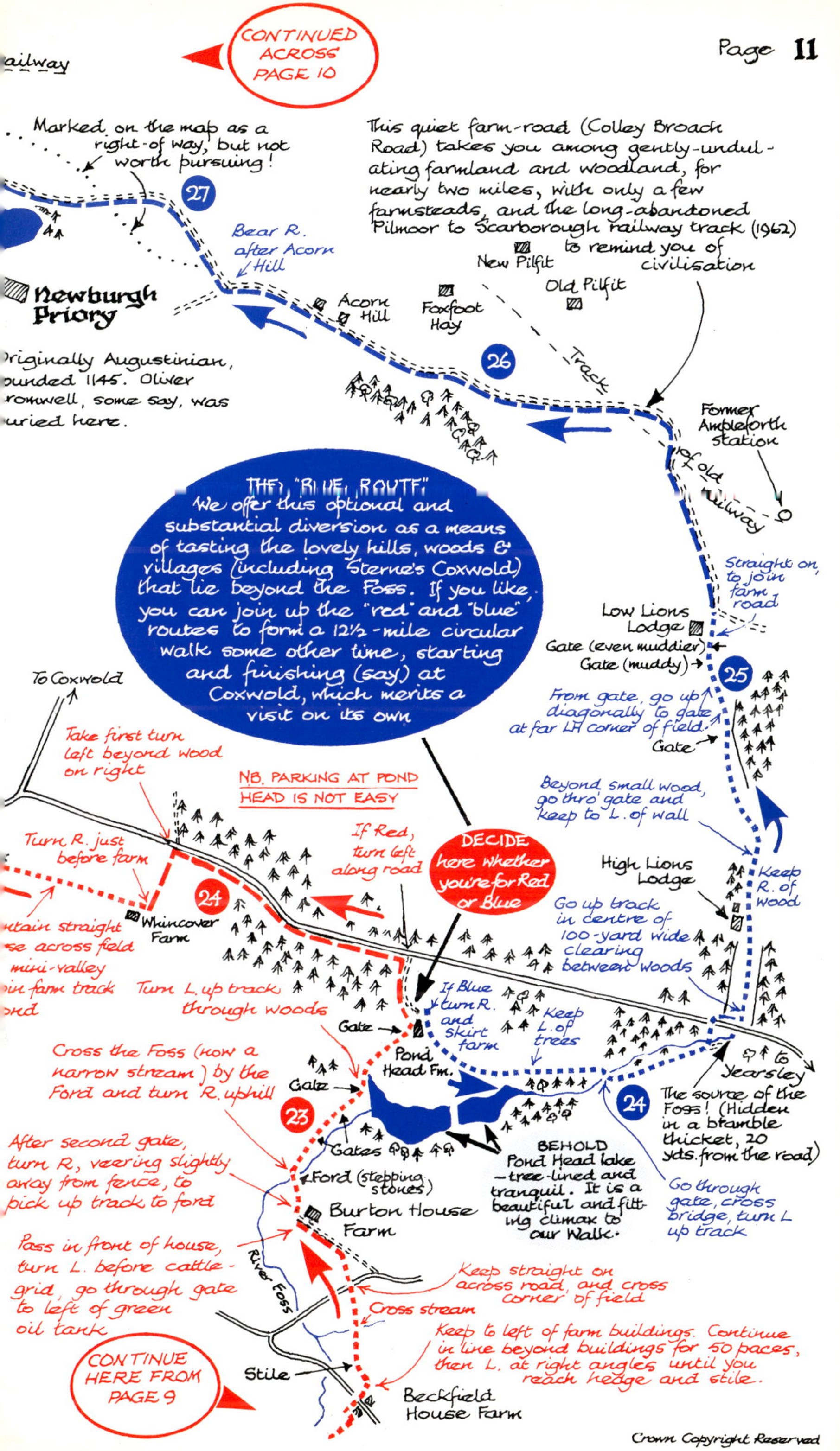

Page **11**

CONTINUED ACROSS PAGE 10

Marked on the map as a right-of-way, but not worth pursuing!

(27)

Bear R. after Acorn Hill

**Newburgh Priory**

Originally Augustinian, founded 1145. Oliver Cromwell, some say, was buried here.

Acorn Hill

New Pilfit    Old Pilfit

Foxfoot Hay

(26)

This quiet farm-road (Colley Broach Road) takes you among gently-undulating farmland and woodland, for nearly two miles, with only a few farmsteads, and the long-abandoned Pilmoor to Scarborough railway track (1962) to remind you of civilisation

Track

Former Ambleforth station
of old railway

Straight on, to join farm road

Low Lions Lodge
Gate (even muddier)
Gate (muddy)

(25)

From gate, go up diagonally to gate at far LH corner of field.
Gate

Beyond small wood, go thro' gate and keep to L. of wall

### THE "BLUE ROUTE"
We offer this optional and substantial diversion as a means of tasting the lovely hills, woods & villages (including Sterne's Coxwold) that lie beyond the Foss. If you like, you can join up the "red" and "blue" routes to form a 12½-mile circular walk some other time, starting and finishing (say) at Coxwold, which merits a visit on its own

To Coxwold

Take first turn left beyond wood on right

Turn R. just before farm

(24) Whincover Farm

tain straight e across field mini-valley farm track nd

Turn L. up track through woods

**NB. PARKING AT POND HEAD IS NOT EASY**

If Red, turn left along road

**DECIDE** here whether you're for Red or Blue

If Blue, turn R. and skirt farm

Gate
Keep L. of trees

High Lions Lodge

Go up track in centre of 100-yard wide clearing between woods

Keep R. of Wood

to Yearsley

Pond Head Fm.

(24)

The source of the Foss! (Hidden in a bramble thicket, 20 yds. from the road)

Cross the Foss (now a narrow stream) by the Ford and turn R. uphill

Gate
Gates
Ford (stepping stones)
Burton House Farm

BEHOLD Pond Head lake — tree-lined and tranquil. It is a beautiful and fitting climax to our walk.

Go through gate, cross bridge, turn L up track

After second gate, turn R, veering slightly away from fence, to pick up track to ford

(23)

Pass in front of house, turn L. before cattle-grid, go through gate to left of green oil tank

River Foss

Keep straight on across road, and cross corner of field

Cross stream

Stile

Beckfield House Farm

Keep to left of farm buildings. Continue in line beyond buildings for 50 paces, then L. at right angles until you reach hedge and stile.

CONTINUE HERE FROM PAGE 9

Crown Copyright Reserved

Page 12

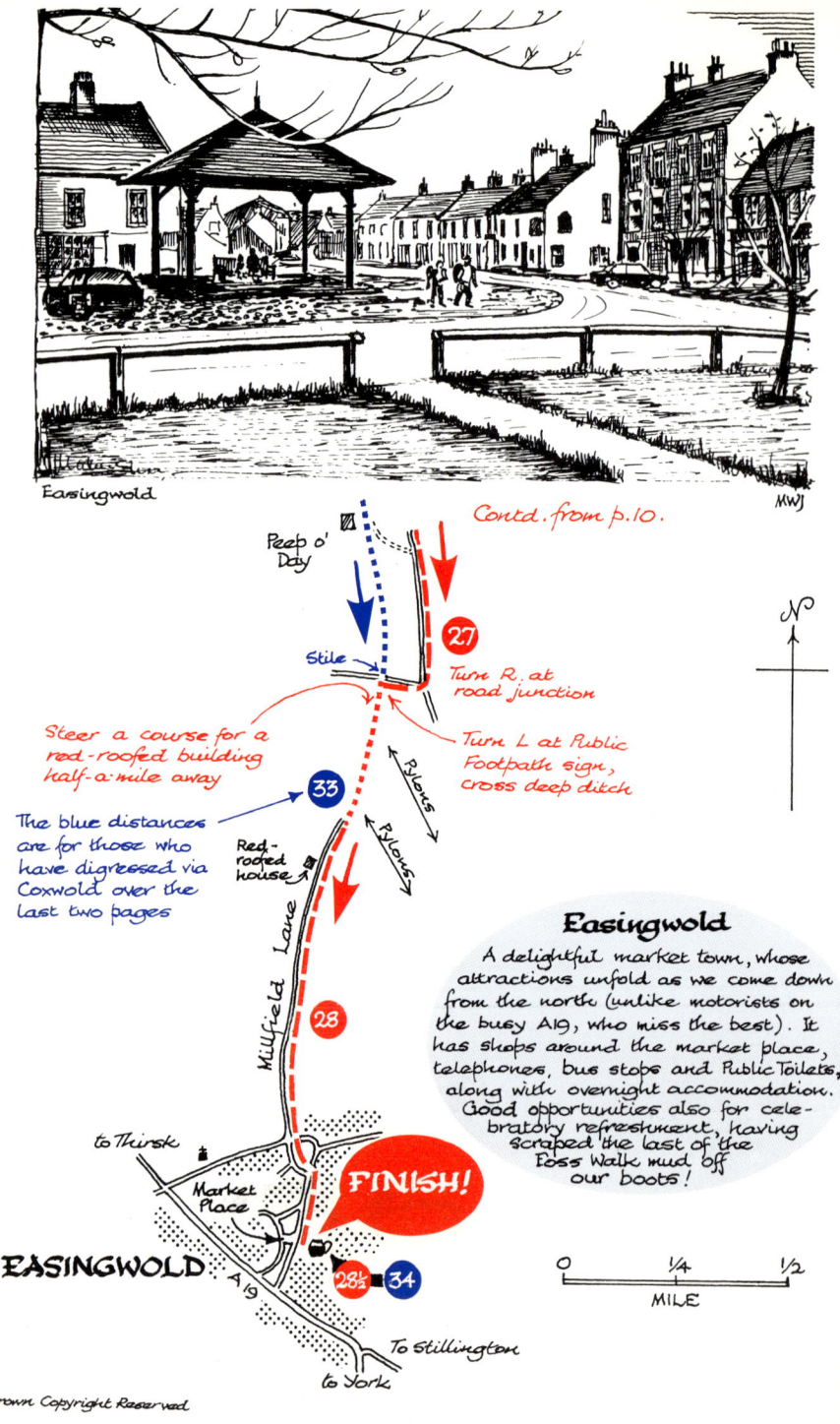

Easingwold

Contd. from p.10.

Peep o' Day

27 Turn R. at road junction

Stile

Steer a course for a red-roofed building half-a-mile away

Turn L at Public Footpath sign, cross deep ditch

33

Pylons

The blue distances are for those who have digressed via Coxwold over the last two pages

Red-roofed house

Pylons

Millfield Lane

28

### Easingwold

A delightful market town, whose attractions unfold as we come down from the north (unlike motorists on the busy A19, who miss the best). It has shops around the market place, telephones, bus stops and Public Toilets, along with overnight accommodation. Good opportunities also for celebratory refreshment, having scraped the last of the Foss Walk mud off our boots!

to Thirsk

Market Place

**FINISH!**

EASINGWOLD  A19

28½  34

To Stillington

to York

0 — ¼ — ½
MILE

Crown Copyright Reserved